_____

to

_____

from

In this journal, you'll find strength and power in God's love and promises straight from Scripture. The prompts and quotes are from (in)courage—a DaySpring community made up of real, authentic, brave women just like you. By going first and sharing our messy hearts and what it looks like to cling to hope, together we become women of courage. Together we can live out our calling as God's daughters.

We hope that your *Take Heart* journal will do just that—become a place where you can cling to the hope of Jesus right in the midst of your chaos and pain.

Take heart, sister. You are not alone.

take heart

A PRAYER JOURNAL

DaySpring

LIVE YOUR FAITH

Truth for Today:

I am a warrior, and God is with me.

1/4/2024

Today I'm grateful for...

my ability to go to PT, to have worship music, my apartment & my job. my family. my health & the finances to get healthy through therapy, PT, etc.

My prayer requests...

- this upcoming semester - peds clinical
- body image (esp. as tif's wedding is coming up)
- relationships - & wanting to do them honoring God. Remove distractions if they're bad & not of you, Lord
- Chase - guide him, Father. Pull him close
- Dad - would you reach him & his heart. Reestablish him as a trustworthy spiritual leader of our home
- Mama - would you be guiding her & speaking tenderly to her.

We live in a fallen, broken world and if we are in a battle it simply means we are warriors.

HOLLEY GERTH

See what great love the Father has lavished on us,
that we should be called children of God!
And that is what we are!

1 JOHN 3:1 NIV

Truth for Today:

I am greatly loved by God, just as I am.

Today I'm grateful for...

1/10/24

that however much space I take up, how I am & how
I act, think, & move in the world, I am as God
made me. & if there's something in me that God
wishes for me to be different, Holy Spirit would
you lead me & prompt me in that way?

My prayer requests...

- clinicals starting on Monday & this crazy semester ahead
- Chase - lead him
- Dad - lead him
- I'd find a church community where I feel seen, heard & loved
- prepare me for a husband
- Help me study & pass the SCKN exam in Feb.
- Jasmine's health
- It's Mina's birthday!
- body image

You are wonderful. You are loved. And when God looks at His creation (that's you! and me!), He says, "It is very good."... and He lavishes His love on us.

MARY CARVER

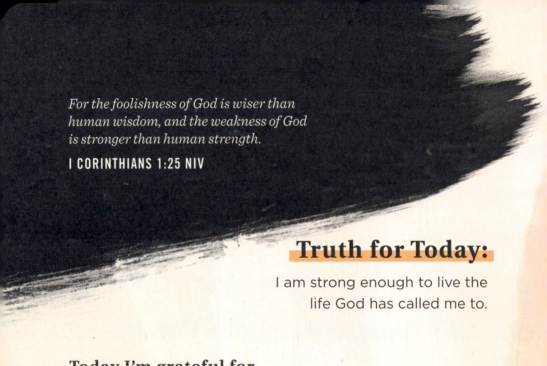

For the foolishness of God is wiser than human wisdom, and the weakness of God is stronger than human strength.

I CORINTHIANS 1:25 NIV

Truth for Today:

I am strong enough to live the
life God has called me to.

Today I'm grateful for...

_____
_____
_____
_____
_____
_____
_____
_____
_____
_____
_____
_____
_____

My prayer requests...

I lack strength, but I have come to know even the weakness of God and His abundant grace is all I need.

ALIA JOY

She gave this name to the Lord who spoke to her:
"You are the God who sees me," for she said,
"I have now seen the One who sees me."

GENESIS 16:13 NIV

Truth for Today:

I am seen by God, even when
I am surrounded by darkness.

Today I'm grateful for...

My prayer requests...

He walks with us in the dark,
guiding us to the light of hope, and He
assures us along the way, "I see you,
I know you, and I love you."

GRACE P. CHO

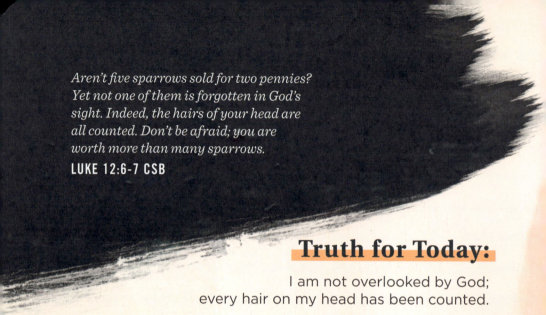

Aren't five sparrows sold for two pennies? Yet not one of them is forgotten in God's sight. Indeed, the hairs of your head are all counted. Don't be afraid; you are worth more than many sparrows.

LUKE 12:6-7 CSB

Truth for Today:

I am not overlooked by God; every hair on my head has been counted.

Today I'm grateful for...

_____

_____

_____

_____

_____

_____

_____

_____

_____

_____

_____

_____

My prayer requests...

God promises that even in
our pain, we matter to Him.
God doesn't overlook us.

ANNA RENDELL

*Like a city whose walls are broken
through is a person who lacks self-control.*

PROVERBS 25:28 NIV

Truth for Today:

I am not powerless; self-control and
boundaries are within my grasp
because of the Holy Spirit in me.

Today I'm grateful for...

_____
_____
_____
_____
_____
_____
_____
_____
_____
_____
_____
_____
_____
_____

My prayer requests...

_It really is okay to set
and keep boundaries.
Good boundaries help us heal._

JENNIFER DUKES LEE

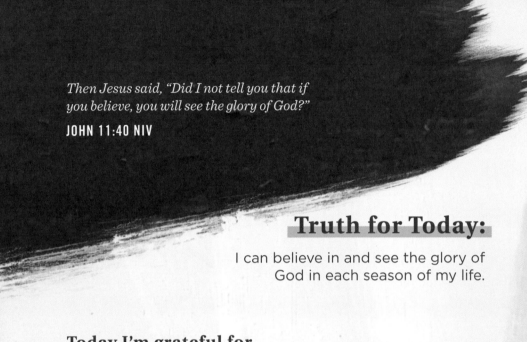

Then Jesus said, "Did I not tell you that if you believe, you will see the glory of God?"

JOHN 11:40 NIV

Truth for Today:

I can believe in and see the glory of God in each season of my life.

Today I'm grateful for...

My prayer requests...

_Glory is the very essence
of God. It's who He is.
It's what makes Him unique._

DORINA LAZO GILMORE

I am in them and You are in Me, so that they may be made completely one, that the world may know You have sent Me and have loved them as You have loved Me.

JOHN 17:23 CSB

Truth for Today:

I can thrive when in unity with God, Jesus, and each other.

Today I'm grateful for...

_____

_____

_____

_____

_____

_____

_____

_____

_____

_____

_____

_____

_____

My prayer requests...

Let's keep showing up
and asking in prayer that
we become united in His love.

LUCRETIA BERRY

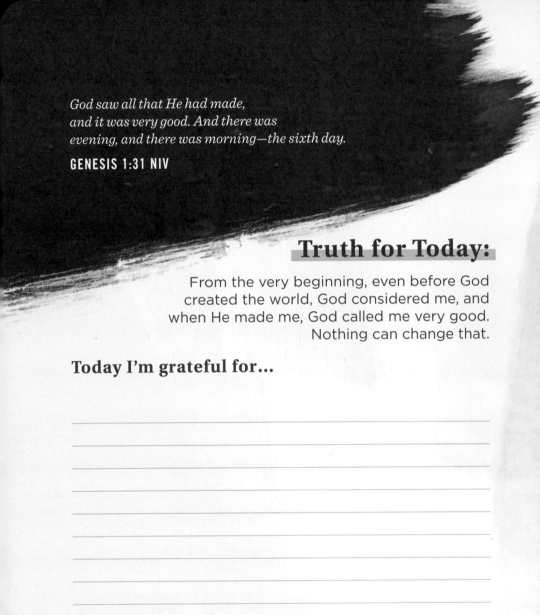

God saw all that He had made,
and it was very good. And there was
evening, and there was morning—the sixth day.

GENESIS 1:31 NIV

Truth for Today:

From the very beginning, even before God
created the world, God considered me, and
when He made me, God called me very good.
Nothing can change that.

Today I'm grateful for...

_____

_____

_____

_____

_____

_____

_____

_____

_____

_____

_____

_____

My prayer requests...

_____
_____
_____
_____
_____
_____
_____
_____
_____
_____
_____
_____
_____
_____
_____
_____
_____
_____

*I've learned what makes us
beautiful to God: the light in our
eyes, the glow on our faces, and
the warmth of our words.*

LIZ CURTIS HIGGS

Let us then with confidence draw near to the throne of grace, that we may receive mercy and find grace to help in time of need.

HEBREWS 4:16 ESV

Truth for Today:

I can confidently share my experiences with God and He will be merciful, offering grace and peace to my heart.

Today I'm grateful for...

_____

_____

_____

_____

_____

_____

_____

_____

_____

_____

_____

_____

_____

My prayer requests...

_Giving voice to our experience
can help unravel the tangle of
shame we're living in._

BECKY KEIFE

He who was seated on the throne said,
"I am making everything new!" Then
He said, "Write this down, for these
words are trustworthy and true."

REVELATION 21:5 NIV

Truth for Today:

I can trust the newness of Christ,
for God says He makes all things new—
including my heart and story. He can resurrect my life.

Today I'm grateful for...

My prayer requests...

Jesus is in the business of making all things new—not perfect, not like they used to be, but new. Third-day-rose-from-the-grave kind of new. Resurrection new.

LISA-JO BAKER

And you will know the truth,
and the truth will set you free.

JOHN 8:32 NLT

Truth for Today:

Jesus is the truth, and He loves me.

Today I'm grateful for...

_____

_____

_____

_____

_____

_____

_____

_____

_____

_____

_____

_____

_____

My prayer requests...

Have courage, friend. You've
got Jesus, who is the Truth.
And the Truth will set you free.

ALIZA LATTA

Even when I go through the darkest valley,
I fear no danger, for You are with me;
Your rod and Your staff—they comfort me.

PSALM 23:4 CSB

Truth for Today:

The Lord will sit with me in my pain and sadness. He will wipe my tears, stroke my hair, and tell me that it won't be like this forever.

Today I'm grateful for...

_____

_____

_____

_____

_____

_____

_____

_____

_____

_____

_____

_____

My prayer requests...

You are never, ever alone.
Jesus is always with us.

JESSICA TURNER

I have said these things to you, that in me you may have peace. In the world you will have tribulation. But take heart; I have overcome the world.

JOHN 16:33 ESV

Truth for Today:

I can take heart, in faith.
Jesus has overcome and so can I!

Today I'm grateful for...

_____

_____

_____

_____

_____

_____

_____

_____

_____

_____

_____

_____

My prayer requests...

_Take heart. Could there be more
beautiful words? Two words that call
my eyes and attention to the heavens,
to hope, to the true Fixer. Take heart._

ANJULI PASCHALL

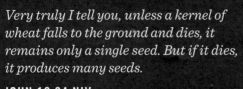

Very truly I tell you, unless a kernel of wheat falls to the ground and dies, it remains only a single seed. But if it dies, it produces many seeds.

JOHN 12:24 NIV

Truth for Today:

God is good in this place,
and He is doing good work in me.

Today I'm grateful for...

My prayer requests...

Like a seed, I am soaking in nutrients through mentoring, counseling, and cultivating life-giving relationships. I'm learning not to fear the dark and instead to embrace this intimate and sacred space with God.

GRACE P. CHO

I have loved you with an everlasting love;
I have drawn you with unfailing kindness.

JEREMIAH 31:3 NIV

Truth for Today:

Jesus sees it all, and loves me so very much.

Today I'm grateful for...

_____
_____
_____
_____
_____
_____
_____
_____
_____
_____
_____
_____

My prayer requests...

Take a deep breath and exhale into the loving arms of Jesus, who holds you and says, "It's okay. I've got you. And I understand you. I will take care of you because you are My beloved."

BONNIE GRAY

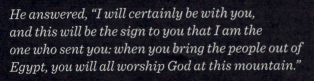

He answered, "I will certainly be with you, and this will be the sign to you that I am the one who sent you: when you bring the people out of Egypt, you will all worship God at this mountain."

EXODUS 3:12 CSB

Truth for Today:

God will answer my prayers in His timing.

Today I'm grateful for...

My prayer requests...

_God really comes through on
His promises and creates new life
in all kinds of beautiful ways._

STEPHANIE BRYANT

Many, LORD my God, are the wonders You have done,
the things You planned for us. None can compare
with You; were I to speak and tell of Your deeds,
they would be too many to declare.

PSALM 40:5 NIV

Truth for Today:

The Lord will meet me here,
right where I am, just as I am.

Today I'm grateful for...

_____
_____
_____
_____
_____
_____
_____
_____
_____
_____
_____
_____
_____

My prayer requests...

We have a God who sits with us in the dark so we can bear witness to the light. A God who will never leave or forsake us and who continues to speak the language of hope into our sorrow.

ALIA JOY

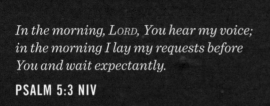

*In the morning, L*ORD*, You hear my voice;*
in the morning I lay my requests before
You and wait expectantly.

PSALM 5:3 NIV

Truth for Today:

God's never not shown up to meet me.

Today I'm grateful for...

_____
_____
_____
_____
_____
_____
_____
_____
_____
_____
_____
_____
_____

My prayer requests...

There's no one-size-fits-all
formula, no right or wrong way to
spend time with Jesus. For me,
I've found nothing better than starting
my day with Scripture open.
Pen to paper. Listening.

BECKY KEIFE

Blessed is the one . . . whose delight is in the law of the LORD, and who meditates on His law day and night. That person is like a tree planted by streams of water, which yields its fruit in season and whose leaf does not wither—whatever they do prospers.

PSALM 1:1–3 NIV

Truth for Today:

God is here with me, ready to fill my heart with peace for the now and hope for the not yet.

Today I'm grateful for...

_____

_____

_____

_____

_____

_____

_____

_____

_____

_____

_____

_____

_____

My prayer requests...

_____
_____
_____
_____
_____
_____
_____
_____
_____
_____
_____
_____
_____
_____
_____
_____
_____
_____

When Jesus is what we seek,
we will find Him in every season.

KARINA ALLEN

Greater love has no one than this:
to lay down one's life for one's friends.

JOHN 15:13 NIV

Truth for Today:

Even in the littlest of things, I can make a difference.
I can lay down my own self for the good of another.

Today I'm grateful for...

_____

_____

_____

_____

_____

_____

_____

_____

_____

_____

_____

_____

My prayer requests...

_____

_____

_____

_____

_____

_____

_____

_____

_____

_____

_____

_____

_____

_____

_____

_____

_____

Take heart. Keep trying.
Even the little things go a long way.

MICHELLE REYES

Be kind and compassionate to one another,
forgiving each other, just as in Christ God forgave you.

EPHESIANS 4:32 NIV

Truth for Today:

I can forgive and be set free from
the hold of anger and hurt.

Today I'm grateful for...

_____

_____

_____

_____

_____

_____

_____

_____

_____

_____

_____

_____

_____

My prayer requests...

Forgiveness is a gift we give ourselves when we offer it to others. In doing so, we don't forgive so we can forget. We forgive so we can be set free.

RENEE SWOPE

"But I will be with you,"
the Lord said to him.

JUDGES 6:16 CSB

Truth for Today:

God is my strength, my anchor, and my peace.
He is with me, and I don't need to be afraid.

Today I'm grateful for...

_____

_____

_____

_____

_____

_____

_____

_____

_____

_____

_____

_____

My prayer requests...

For me, taking heart looks like believing in and leaning on the God who demolishes fear.

ANNA RENDELL

Finally, all of you should be of one mind.
Sympathize with each other. Love each other
as brothers and sisters. Be tenderhearted,
and keep a humble attitude.
1 PETER 3:8 NLT

Truth for Today:

I can be kind, tenderhearted, and humble.

Today I'm grateful for...

_____
_____
_____
_____
_____
_____
_____
_____
_____
_____
_____
_____

My prayer requests...

God wants us to be His hands
and feet, and extend compassion.
JENNIFER UECKERT

But you are a chosen people, a royal priesthood, a holy nation, God's special possession, that you may declare the praises of Him who called you out of darkness into His wonderful light. Once you were not a people, but now you are the people of God; once you had not received mercy, but now you have received mercy.

1 PETER 2:9–10 NIV

Truth for Today:

I am chosen by God—royal too!
I am God's own—valuable and priceless.

Today I'm grateful for...

_____

_____

_____

_____

_____

_____

_____

_____

_____

_____

My prayer requests...

We must know God for ourselves—
hearing God sing over us, calling us
by His own name. God's people. God's
creation. God's beloved.

PATRICIA RAYBON

God, the Master, told the dry bones,
"Watch this: I'm bringing the breath
of life to you and you'll come to life."

EZEKIEL 37:5 THE MESSAGE

Truth for Today:

God will breathe new life into me.

Today I'm grateful for...

_____

_____

_____

_____

_____

_____

_____

_____

_____

_____

_____

_____

My prayer requests...

Let's ask God to breathe new life into our dry bones, and then watch in believing expectation.

BECKY KEIFE

She turned to leave and saw someone standing there. It was Jesus, but she didn't recognize Him. "Dear woman, why are you crying?" Jesus asked her. "Who are you looking for?" She thought He was the gardener. "Sir," she said, "if you have taken Him away, tell me where you have put Him, and I will go and get Him." "Mary!" Jesus said. She turned to Him and cried out, "Rabboni!" (which is Hebrew for "Teacher").

JOHN 20:14–16 NLT

Truth for Today:

I am free to show up exactly as I am, with my grief, doubt, confusion, and fears.

Today I'm grateful for...

_____
_____
_____
_____
_____
_____
_____
_____
_____
_____
_____
_____

My prayer requests...

Jesus meets us in our mourning and sees us in our sadness. His tone is gentle and kind, patient and loving.

KAITLYN BOUCHILLON

She is clothed with strength and dignity;
she can laugh at the days to come.

PROVERBS 31:25 NIV

Truth for Today:

I can find joy in the worst of circumstances,
and I trust God to handle it all.

Today I'm grateful for...

_____

_____

_____

_____

_____

_____

_____

_____

_____

_____

_____

_____

_____

My prayer requests...

I'm learning the gift of laughter.
MICHELE CUSHATT

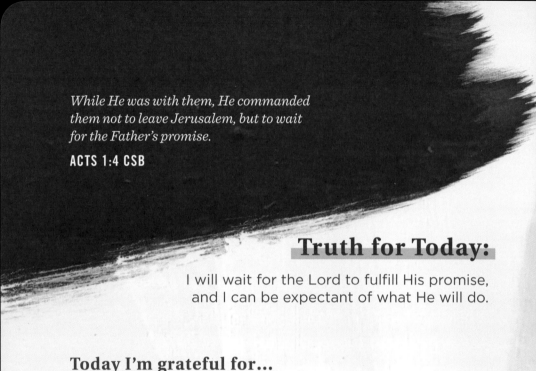

While He was with them, He commanded them not to leave Jerusalem, but to wait for the Father's promise.

ACTS 1:4 CSB

Truth for Today:

I will wait for the Lord to fulfill His promise, and I can be expectant of what He will do.

Today I'm grateful for...

_____

_____

_____

_____

_____

_____

_____

_____

_____

_____

_____

_____

_____

My prayer requests...

_Nothing beats the life-giving
abundance that comes from choosing
to be deeply rooted and invested right
where God has us—in our Jerusalem._

JEN SCHMIDT

But blessed is the one who trusts in the LORD, whose confidence is in Him.

JEREMIAH 17:7 NIV

Truth for Today:

I am blessed because I trust in the Lord and have confidence in Jesus.

Today I'm grateful for...

_____

_____

_____

_____

_____

_____

_____

_____

_____

_____

_____

_____

My prayer requests...

_____

_____

_____

_____

_____

_____

_____

_____

_____

_____

_____

_____

_____

_____

_____

_____

God wants all of us to
experience His abundance.
DORINA LAZO GILMORE

Blessed be the God and Father of our Lord Jesus Christ, who has blessed us in Christ with every spiritual blessing in the heavenly places, even as he chose us in him before the foundation of the world, that we should be holy and blameless before him.

EPHESIANS 1:3–4 ESV

Truth for Today:

I am a beloved child of God, lavished with blessings, and chosen for a purpose.

Today I'm grateful for...

_____

_____

_____

_____

_____

_____

_____

_____

_____

_____

_____

My prayer requests...

We are beloved daughters of the King of kings, worthy, significant, and more than adequate because of Jesus in us.

ROBIN DANCE

And he told them . . . that they ought always to pray and not lose heart.

LUKE 18:1 ESV

Truth for Today:

I can pray with all my heart, and trust the Healer at work.

Today I'm grateful for...

_____
_____
_____
_____
_____
_____
_____
_____
_____
_____
_____
_____

My prayer requests...

*Nothing is too far
gone for Jesus to move.*

KRISTEN STRONG

Instead He emptied Himself by assuming the form of a servant, taking on the likeness of humanity. And when He had come as a man, He humbled Himself by becoming obedient to the point of death—even to death on a cross.

PHILIPPIANS 2:7–8 CSB

Truth for Today:

I can love deep, and wide, and long, and high—as I have been loved.

Today I'm grateful for...

_____

_____

_____

_____

_____

_____

_____

_____

_____

_____

_____

_____

_____

My prayer requests...

*Love means showing up,
speaking up, and sticking around.*

GRACE P. CHO

And let us consider one another to provoke love and good works, not neglecting to gather together, as some are in the habit of doing, but encouraging each other, and all the more as you see the day approaching.

HEBREWS 10:24-25 CSB

Truth for Today:

I can look out for the people around me, encouraging them in love.

Today I'm grateful for...

_____
_____
_____
_____
_____
_____
_____
_____
_____
_____
_____

My prayer requests...

_____

_____

_____

_____

_____

_____

_____

_____

_____

_____

_____

_____

_____

_____

_____

_____

_____

*We can hold strong to Jesus,
knowing that God is redeeming His
body, His bride, until Christ returns.*

DAWN CAMP

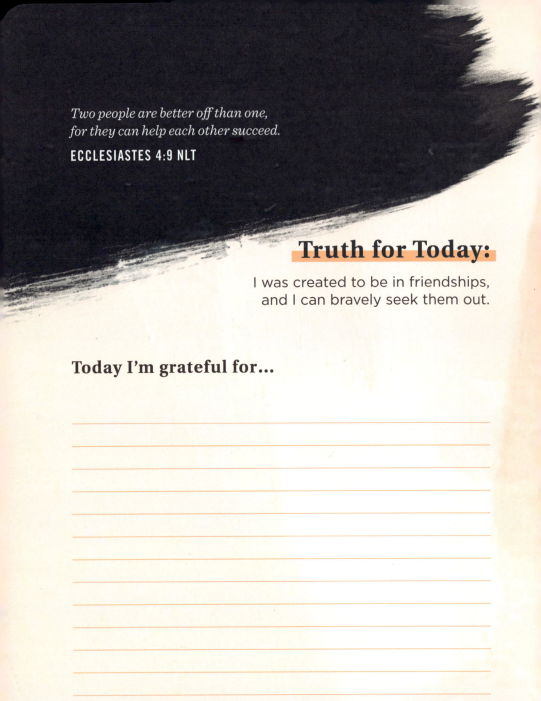

Two people are better off than one,
for they can help each other succeed.

ECCLESIASTES 4:9 NLT

Truth for Today:

I was created to be in friendships,
and I can bravely seek them out.

Today I'm grateful for...

My prayer requests...

We need backup. Encouragers. Help.
We weren't meant to mother alone.

ANNA RENDELL

And not only that, but we also rejoice in our afflictions, because we know that affliction produces endurance, endurance produces proven character, and proven character produces hope. This hope will not disappoint us, because God's love has been poured out in our hearts through the Holy Spirit who was given to us.

ROMANS 5:3–5 CSB

Truth for Today:

I can place my hope in Christ and know that I won't be disappointed.

Today I'm grateful for...

_____

_____

_____

_____

_____

_____

_____

_____

_____

_____

_____

_____

My prayer requests...

Hope is not about what isn't.
Hope is always about what isn't yet.
DEIDRA RIGGS

Those who plant in tears will harvest with shouts of joy. They weep as they go to plant their seed, but they sing as they return with the harvest.

PSALM 126:5–6 NLT

Truth for Today:

What I cry about today may be what I rejoice over in time.

Today I'm grateful for...

_____

_____

_____

_____

_____

_____

_____

_____

_____

_____

_____

_____

My prayer requests...

_____
_____
_____
_____
_____
_____
_____
_____
_____
_____
_____
_____
_____
_____
_____

*Let's dare to believe that our
tears are not really about an ending
but instead, somehow, a beginning.
And there is beauty coming.*

HOLLEY GERTH

So be strong and courageous! Do not be afraid and do not panic before them. For the Lord your God will personally go ahead of you. He will neither fail you nor abandon you.

DEUTERONOMY 31:6 NLT

Truth for Today:

I am courageous enough to take the next step in faith, because God goes before me and I am not abandoned.

Today I'm grateful for...

_____

_____

_____

_____

_____

_____

_____

_____

_____

_____

_____

_____

My prayer requests...

_Your bravery comes from truth and
the ability to listen to God's voice._

STEPHANIE BRYANT

Again, the kingdom of heaven is like a merchant looking for fine pearls. When he found one of great value, he went away and sold everything he had and bought it.

MATTHEW 13:45–46 NIV

Truth for Today:

I cling to the hope that something good is coming, that something good will be produced from the grit and struggle, that there will be treasure to behold after this hardship.

Today I'm grateful for...

_____

_____

_____

_____

_____

_____

_____

_____

_____

_____

_____

My prayer requests...

Struggle is a part of living,
but when we know we are
producing something good,
it can help us through it.

KRISTEN WELCH

The LORD is near the brokenhearted;
He saves those crushed in spirit.

PSALM 34:18 CSB

Truth for Today:

The Lord is near me, no matter what.

Today I'm grateful for...

_____

_____

_____

_____

_____

_____

_____

_____

_____

_____

_____

My prayer requests...

God promises to be with the brokenhearted. Period. No restrictions or expiration dates. No exclusions or requirements. Just love and comfort.

MARY CARVER

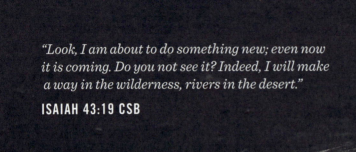

"Look, I am about to do something new; even now it is coming. Do you not see it? Indeed, I will make a way in the wilderness, rivers in the desert."

ISAIAH 43:19 CSB

Truth for Today:

If this is the end of one thing, it could truly be the beginning of another.

Today I'm grateful for...

_____

_____

_____

_____

_____

_____

_____

_____

_____

_____

_____

_____

_____

My prayer requests...

God promises something new,
even now. He always makes a way.

ROBIN DANCE

You intended to harm me, but God intended it for good to accomplish what is now being done, the saving of many lives.

GENESIS 50:20 NIV

Truth for Today:

I can give thanks for God allowing this unexpected journey.

Today I'm grateful for...

_____
_____
_____
_____
_____
_____
_____
_____
_____
_____
_____
_____

My prayer requests...

What life intends for evil,
God will turn into good.
PATRICIA RAYBON

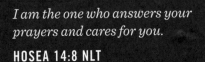

I am the one who answers your prayers and cares for you.

HOSEA 14:8 NLT

Truth for Today:

God truly, deeply, wholly cares for me.

Today I'm grateful for...

My prayer requests...

Alone doesn't exist within the bounds of God's love for you.

SHANNAN MARTIN

You go before me and follow me.
You place Your hand of blessing on my head.

PSALM 139:5 NLT

Truth for Today:

God goes before me to make a way and clear a path.
He sticks with me, a constant friend and guide.

Today I'm grateful for...

_____

_____

_____

_____

_____

_____

_____

_____

_____

_____

_____

_____

My prayer requests...

_____

_____

_____

_____

_____

_____

_____

_____

_____

_____

_____

_____

_____

_____

_____

_____

_____

Seasons change but God remains.

KAITLYN BOUCHILLON

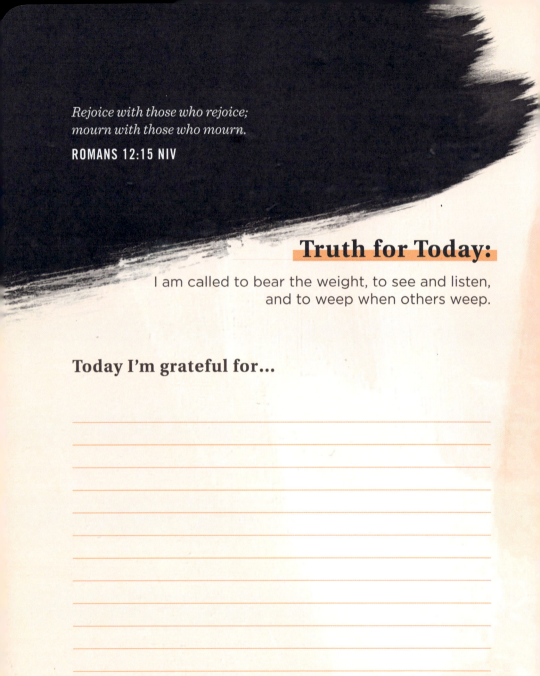

Rejoice with those who rejoice;
mourn with those who mourn.

ROMANS 12:15 NIV

Truth for Today:

I am called to bear the weight, to see and listen,
and to weep when others weep.

Today I'm grateful for...

My prayer requests...

_What if we let the tears
flow and stopped putting
a time limit on grief?_

GRACE P. CHO

"Are You the Messiah we've been expecting, or should we keep looking for someone else?"

MATTHEW 11:3 NLT

Truth for Today:

In my doubt, I am brought closer to God's heart.

Today I'm grateful for...

_____
_____
_____
_____
_____
_____
_____
_____
_____
_____
_____
_____

My prayer requests...

_____

_____

_____

_____

_____

_____

_____

_____

_____

_____

_____

_____

_____

_____

_____

_____

_____

*Grace always weaves its
way in and through the
wreckage and the wounds.
Doubt doesn't mean disbelief.*

TASHA JUN

Have I not commanded you? Be strong and courageous. Do not be afraid; do not be discouraged, for the LORD your God will be with you wherever you go.

JOSHUA 1:9 NIV

Truth for Today:

I am a warrior, and with God's power and grace, I will make it.

Today I'm grateful for...

_____

_____

_____

_____

_____

_____

_____

_____

_____

_____

_____

_____

My prayer requests...

_____
_____
_____
_____
_____
_____
_____
_____
_____
_____
_____
_____
_____
_____
_____
_____
_____
_____

Because God is with you,
you will have your own victory.

S. G. WILLOUGHBY

God said to Moses, "I AM WHO I AM.
This is what you are to say to the Israelites:
'I AM has sent Me to you.'"

EXODUS 3:14 NIV

Truth for Today:

I am more than my circumstances,
because I am with the great I AM.

Today I'm grateful for...

_____
_____
_____
_____
_____
_____
_____
_____
_____
_____
_____
_____
_____

My prayer requests...

We don't have to journey alone.
We get to coauthor our own stories.

LUCRETIA BERRY

He heals the brokenhearted and bandages their wounds. He counts the number of the stars; He gives names to all of them.

PSALM 147:3 CSB

Truth for Today:

I am broken. I am needy. I can't fix myself. And that's where I see the incredible beauty of God's grace.

Today I'm grateful for...

_____

_____

_____

_____

_____

_____

_____

_____

_____

_____

_____

_____

My prayer requests...

_____

_____

_____

_____

_____

_____

_____

_____

_____

_____

_____

_____

_____

_____

_____

_____

_____

_____

There is hope in the
broken and needy places.
LISA LEONARD

Love the Lord your God with all your heart and with all your soul and with all your mind and with all your strength. The second is this: "Love your neighbor as yourself."

MARK 12:30–31 NIV

Truth for Today:

I will love God and God's people with my whole heart.

Today I'm grateful for...

_____

_____

_____

_____

_____

_____

_____

_____

_____

_____

_____

_____

_____

My prayer requests...

_____

_____

_____

_____

_____

_____

_____

_____

_____

_____

_____

_____

_____

_____

_____

_____

_____

Loving ourselves has a positive ripple effect on our families, jobs, communities, and the world.

JESSICA TURNER

*You have searched me, L*ORD*, and You know me.*
You know when I sit and when I rise; You perceive
my thoughts from afar. You discern my going out
and my lying down; You are familiar with all my ways.

PSALM 139:1–3 NIV

Truth for Today:

I am seen. I am not alone.

Today I'm grateful for...

My prayer requests...

God sees you, friend. Always.
BECKY KEIFE

Build homes, and plan to stay. Plant gardens, and eat the food they produce. . . . And work for the peace and prosperity of the city where I sent you into exile. Pray to the Lord for it, for its welfare will determine your welfare.

JEREMIAH 29:5, 7 NLT

Truth for Today:

I can learn how to be still and how to receive, with hands open to God's plan.

Today I'm grateful for...

_____

_____

_____

_____

_____

_____

_____

_____

_____

_____

_____

_____

_____

_____

My prayer requests...

_____

_____

_____

_____

_____

_____

_____

_____

_____

_____

_____

_____

_____

_____

_____

_____

_____

_____

_____

*The death of my dream was not
the death of God's dreams for me.*

TASHA JUN

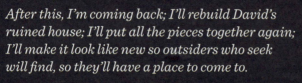

After this, I'm coming back; I'll rebuild David's ruined house; I'll put all the pieces together again; I'll make it look like new so outsiders who seek will find, so they'll have a place to come to.

ACTS 15:16, 17 THE MESSAGE

Truth for Today:

I will remember that there's always room at the table God chooses for me.

Today I'm grateful for...

My prayer requests...

As we pray for God to show us where we belong, let us be on the outside looking up.

KRISTEN STRONG

But seek His kingdom, and these things will be given to you as well.

LUKE 12:31 NIV

Truth for Today:

I can stand with arms open and heart ready to hear from Jesus alone.

Today I'm grateful for...

_____

_____

_____

_____

_____

_____

_____

_____

_____

_____

_____

_____

My prayer requests...

_____

_____

_____

_____

_____

_____

_____

_____

_____

_____

_____

_____

_____

_____

_____

*Jesus promises us that if we strive
for His kingdom, everything else
that's truly important "will be
given to you."*

JENNIFER DUKES LEE

Two are better than one because they have a good reward for their efforts. For if either falls, his companion can lift him up; but pity the one who falls without another to lift him up. Also, if two lie down together, they can keep warm; but how can one person alone keep warm? And if someone overpowers one person, two can resist him. A cord of three strands is not easily broken.

ECCLESIASTES 4:9–12 CSB

Truth for Today:

I was created for community,
and I do not have to do life alone.

Today I'm grateful for...

_____

_____

_____

_____

_____

_____

_____

_____

_____

_____

_____

_____

My prayer requests...

As the storms of life crash,
we can huddle together face-to-face
with our Savior at the helm.

JEN SCHMIDT

Every good gift and every perfect gift is
from above, coming down from the Father.

JAMES 1:17 ESV

Truth for Today:

Even when nothing else around us is good, God's presence
in the midst of our deepest pain is a good gift indeed.

Today I'm grateful for...

_____

_____

_____

_____

_____

_____

_____

_____

_____

_____

_____

_____

My prayer requests...

_____

_____

_____

_____

_____

_____

_____

_____

_____

_____

_____

_____

_____

_____

_____

_____

_____

_____

*Even in my insurmountable grief,
there is good. There is always good
because there is always God.*

ALIZA LATTA

*"For My thoughts are not your thoughts,
neither are your ways My ways," declares
the Lord. "As the heavens are higher than the
earth, so are My ways higher than your ways
and My thoughts than your thoughts."*

ISAIAH 55:8–9 NIV

Truth for Today:

God has everything under control. He will bring
perspective to every confusing and unclear situation.

Today I'm grateful for...

My prayer requests...

*There is a larger meaning
to our journey, and
nothing is ever wasted.*

JENNIFER UECKERT

In the same way the Spirit also helps us in our weakness, because we do not know what to pray for as we should, but the Spirit Himself intercedes for us with inexpressible groanings.

ROMANS 8:26 CSB

Truth for Today:

Even when I don't know what or how to pray, the Holy Spirit intercedes on my behalf.

Today I'm grateful for...

_____

_____

_____

_____

_____

_____

_____

_____

_____

_____

_____

_____

_____

My prayer requests...

_I've learned that worry solves nothing,
but prayer can change everything._

DAWN CAMP

Come away by yourselves to a secluded place and rest a while.

MARK 6:31 NASB

Truth for Today:

I can rest in God's love.

Today I'm grateful for...

My prayer requests...

What if God's plan for us is not
to be busier but to be more loved?
Hear God whisper to you today,
You are beautiful to Me. Come away
with Me and rest awhile.

BONNIE GRAY

I wait for the L<small>ORD</small>, my whole being waits,
and in His word I put my hope

PSALM 130:5 NIV

Truth for Today:

I can trust God with hope because
He never changes, and His love is unconditional.

Today I'm grateful for...

_____

_____

_____

_____

_____

_____

_____

_____

_____

_____

_____

_____

_____

My prayer requests...

_God's goodness is real and
steadfast. It's for me.
It's for you. It's for the world._
KARINA ALLEN

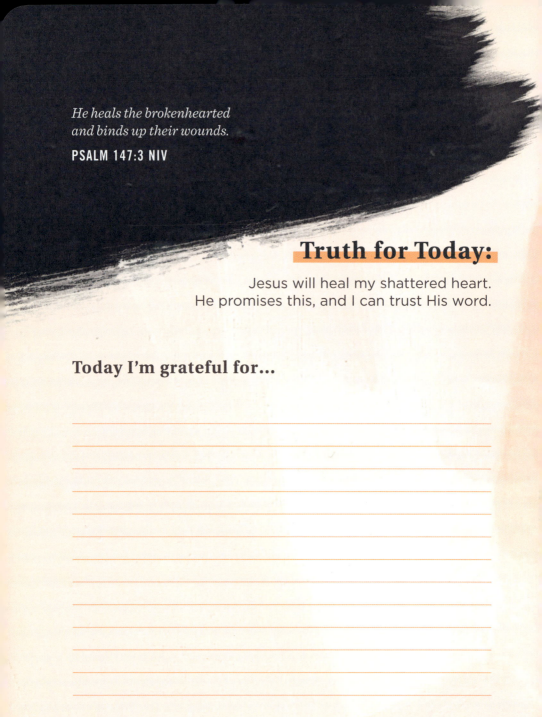

He heals the brokenhearted
and binds up their wounds.

PSALM 147:3 NIV

Truth for Today:

Jesus will heal my shattered heart.
He promises this, and I can trust His word.

Today I'm grateful for...

My prayer requests...

_Jesus heals your wounds—not just
with time but entirely with His own
brokenness—to make you whole._

JENNIFER DUKES LEE

For I am convinced that neither death nor life,
neither angels nor demons, neither the present
nor the future, nor any powers, neither height nor
depth, nor anything else in all creation, will be able
to separate us from the love of God that is in Christ
Jesus our Lord.

ROMANS 8:38–39 NIV

Truth for Today:

I can cling to what is true: that God has not abandoned me, that my greatest hope is unchanging, that God is sure and lasting, and that I am unable to be separated from Him.

Today I'm grateful for...

_____

_____

_____

_____

_____

_____

_____

_____

_____

_____

_____

_____

_____

My prayer requests...

_____
_____
_____
_____
_____
_____
_____
_____
_____
_____
_____
_____
_____
_____
_____
_____

*Life can be terribly hard
and God can still be good.*

ELIZABETH MANLEY

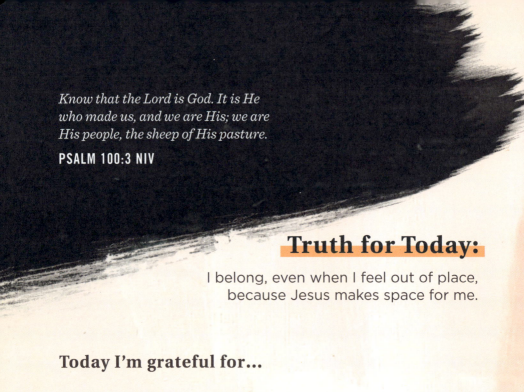

Know that the Lord is God. It is He who made us, and we are His; we are His people, the sheep of His pasture.

PSALM 100:3 NIV

Truth for Today:

I belong, even when I feel out of place, because Jesus makes space for me.

Today I'm grateful for...

_____

_____

_____

_____

_____

_____

_____

_____

_____

_____

_____

_____

My prayer requests...

_____

_____

_____

_____

_____

_____

_____

_____

_____

_____

_____

_____

_____

_____

_____

_____

_____

_____

*In Christ, my identity belongs
to something larger than me.*

MICHELLE REYES

Don't worry about anything; instead, pray about everything. Tell God what you need, and thank Him for all He has done. Then you will experience God's peace, which exceeds anything we can understand. His peace will guard your hearts and minds as you live in Christ Jesus.

PHILIPPIANS 4:6–7 NLT

Truth for Today:

I can take a break from worrying, pressing the pause button on the concerns that consume me, because God will give me what I need.

Today I'm grateful for...

_____

_____

_____

_____

_____

_____

_____

_____

_____

_____

_____

_____

My prayer requests...

_____

_____

_____

_____

_____

_____

_____

_____

_____

_____

_____

_____

_____

_____

_____

_____

_____

*God is there, waiting to
give you all you need.*

RENEE SWOPE

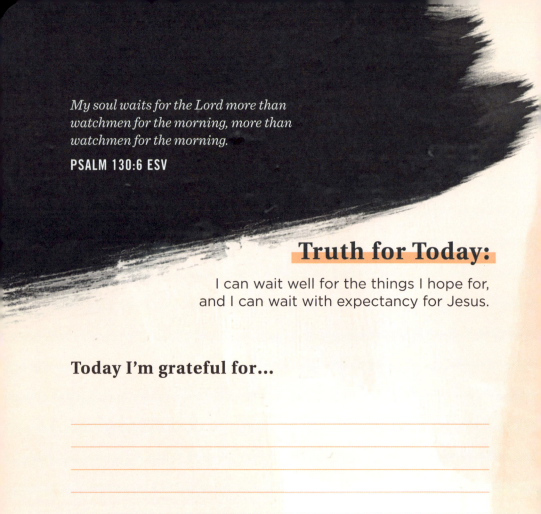

My soul waits for the Lord more than watchmen for the morning, more than watchmen for the morning.

PSALM 130:6 ESV

Truth for Today:

I can wait well for the things I hope for, and I can wait with expectancy for Jesus.

Today I'm grateful for...

My prayer requests...

Even if my relationship status never changes, my Christ will always be near, and that will always be a commitment worth remembering and a relationship worth investing in.

MELISSA ZALDIVAR

I appeal to you therefore, brothers, by the mercies of God, to present your bodies as a living sacrifice, holy and acceptable to God, which is your spiritual worship. Do not be conformed to this world, but be transformed by the renewal of your mind, that by testing you may discern what is the will of God, what is good and acceptable and perfect.

ROMANS 12:1–2 ESV

Truth for Today:

My identity is complex and good, because God created me in His image.

Today I'm grateful for...

_____

_____

_____

_____

_____

_____

_____

_____

_____

_____

_____

_____

My prayer requests...

_Jesus, our resurrected King,
resurrects and renews the
assimilated parts of our identity._

TASHA JUN

*Be strong in the Lord
and in His mighty power.*

EPHESIANS 6:10 NIV

Truth for Today:

When I'm in the thick of a battle unseen,
God will provide armor and peace.

Today I'm grateful for...

_____

_____

_____

_____

_____

_____

_____

_____

_____

_____

_____

_____

My prayer requests...

Sometimes taking heart in the
hard means taking into account
the battles we feel but cannot see.

BECKY KEIFE

*Give all your worries and cares
to God, for He cares about you.*

1 PETER 5:7 NLT

Truth for Today:

God is the Fixer, the Healer,
the Burden Bearer...and I don't have to be.

Today I'm grateful for...

_____
_____
_____
_____
_____
_____
_____
_____
_____
_____
_____
_____
_____
_____

My prayer requests...

_To believe that God is the
Healer and the Burden Bearer
brings healing to my life._

AMBER C. HAINES

Blessed are the poor in spirit,
for theirs is the kingdom of heaven.

MATTHEW 5:3 NIV

Truth for Today:

The Lord will meet me in my places of weakness.

Today I'm grateful for...

_____
_____
_____
_____
_____
_____
_____
_____
_____
_____
_____
_____

My prayer requests...

*Even when we think we
have nothing to offer, Jesus is
the blessing that meets us
in our poverty.*

ALIA JOY

For your Maker is your husband, the LORD of hosts is his name; and the Holy One of Israel is your Redeemer, the God of the whole earth he is called.

ISAIAH 54:5 ESV

Truth for Today:

I don't have to be alone;
God is always and forever by my side.

Today I'm grateful for...

_____

_____

_____

_____

_____

_____

_____

_____

_____

_____

_____

_____

My prayer requests...

God transforms even the darkest
circumstances for His glory.

DORINA LAZO GILMORE

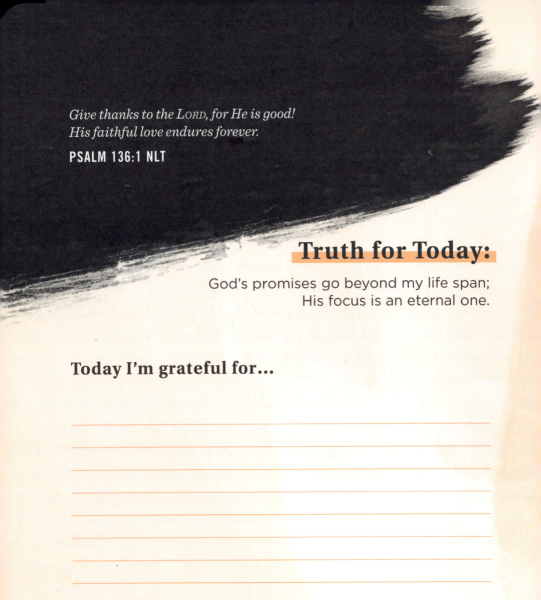

*Give thanks to the L*ORD, *for He is good!*
His faithful love endures forever.

PSALM 136:1 NLT

Truth for Today:

God's promises go beyond my life span;
His focus is an eternal one.

Today I'm grateful for...

My prayer requests...

_Even if my prayers aren't answered
on this side of the pearly gates,
they will certainly receive a
glorious answer in eternity._

BEV RIHTARCHIK

Why am I discouraged? Why is my
heart so sad? I will put my hope in God!
I will praise Him again—my Savior and my God!

PSALM 42:5 NLT

Truth for Today:

I can call God good, even when
I'm feeling both hurt and hope.

Today I'm grateful for...

_____

_____

_____

_____

_____

_____

_____

_____

_____

_____

_____

_____

My prayer requests...

We don't have to be afraid of hurt or afraid to hope. They are both part of what makes us who we are, part of our beauty and strength and scars.

HOLLEY GERTH

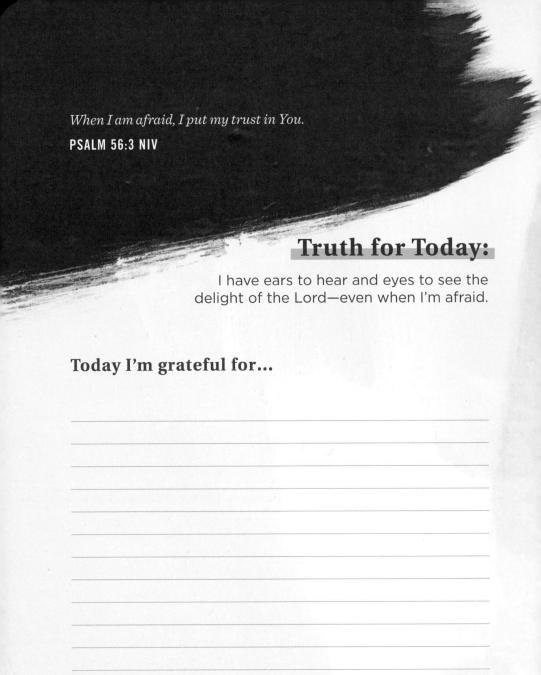

When I am afraid, I put my trust in You.

PSALM 56:3 NIV

Truth for Today:

I have ears to hear and eyes to see the delight of the Lord—even when I'm afraid.

Today I'm grateful for...

My prayer requests...

I am looking for Jesus in all the surprising ways that He may show up on the playground of life, because He's already with us, beckoning our notice.

JOANNE MOON

I will sing about the L<small>ORD</small>'s faithful love forever; I will proclaim your faithfulness to all generations with my mouth.

PSALM 89:1 CSB

Truth for Today:

Throughout transitions and new beginnings, God is still faithful.

Today I'm grateful for...

_____

_____

_____

_____

_____

_____

_____

_____

_____

_____

_____

_____

_____

_____

_____

My prayer requests...

As we exit one season and enter a new one, in the transition pay attention to the things that pull at your heart, to the areas of your life that may need more care, and don't be afraid to start planning and dreaming.

DAWN CAMP

He has made everything beautiful in its time.

ECCLESIASTES 3:11 NIV

Truth for Today:

God has made all things beautiful—
including me—and I can see evidence of
His beauty and handiwork all around me.

Today I'm grateful for...

My prayer requests...

Scripture says that God has
made everything beautiful.
Seeing life through that lens is
profound and life-giving.

JESSICA TURNER

We know that all things work together
for the good of those who love God,
who are called according to His purpose.

ROMANS 8:28 CSB

Truth for Today:

I can trust that He is a good God,
a loving Father who gives good gifts to His children.

Today I'm grateful for...

_____

_____

_____

_____

_____

_____

_____

_____

_____

_____

_____

_____

My prayer requests...

The truth is clear: God redeems every last thing. He is a way-making, promise-keeping, battle-winning, water-walking, storm-stilling, faithful Friend and Savior.

KAITLYN BOUCHILLON

So the heavens and the earth and everything in them were completed. On the seventh day God had completed His work that He had done, and He rested on the seventh day from all His work that He had done. God blessed the seventh day and declared it holy, for on it He rested from all His work of creation.

GENESIS 2:1–3 CSB

Truth for Today:

God modeled rest and I can follow His example.

Today I'm grateful for...

_____
_____
_____
_____
_____
_____
_____
_____
_____
_____
_____
_____
_____

My prayer requests...

Real self-care, the kind that actually takes care of one's self, is Scriptural.

ANNA E. RENDELL

Trust in the Lord with all your heart; do not depend on your own understanding. Seek His will in all you do, and He will show you which path to take.

PROVERBS 3:5–6 NLT

Truth for Today:

God's way is love, and walking in love can be one way I trust Him.

Today I'm grateful for...

My prayer requests...

I want to tell you, God's got this.
He does. So go ahead and breathe.

DEIDRA RIGGS

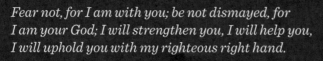

Fear not, for I am with you; be not dismayed, for I am your God; I will strengthen you, I will help you, I will uphold you with my righteous right hand.

ISAIAH 41:10 ESV

Truth for Today:

God is with me, ready to strengthen, help, and uphold my heart.

Today I'm grateful for...

_____

_____

_____

_____

_____

_____

_____

_____

_____

_____

_____

_____

_____

My prayer requests...

_When you cannot stand on your own,
when your faith and strength fail you,
God will be right there to prop you up
and propel you forward. He promises
to help us and to hold us, and He will._

MARY CARVER

I am the vine; you are the branches.
If you remain in Me and I in you,
you will bear much fruit; apart from
Me you can do nothing.

JOHN 15:5 NIV

Truth for Today:

If I remain in Jesus, I can still bear much fruit,
even in difficult seasons of life.

Today I'm grateful for...

_____
_____
_____
_____
_____
_____
_____
_____
_____
_____
_____
_____
_____

My prayer requests...

_____
_____
_____
_____
_____
_____
_____
_____
_____
_____
_____
_____
_____
_____
_____
_____
_____

*When all the striving, all the gifts,
all the callings and passions are set
aside, and when all that remains is only
Jesus, take heart. You're not lost. You're
not without purpose. Stay near and
abide in Christ, and that is enough.*

GRACE P. CHO

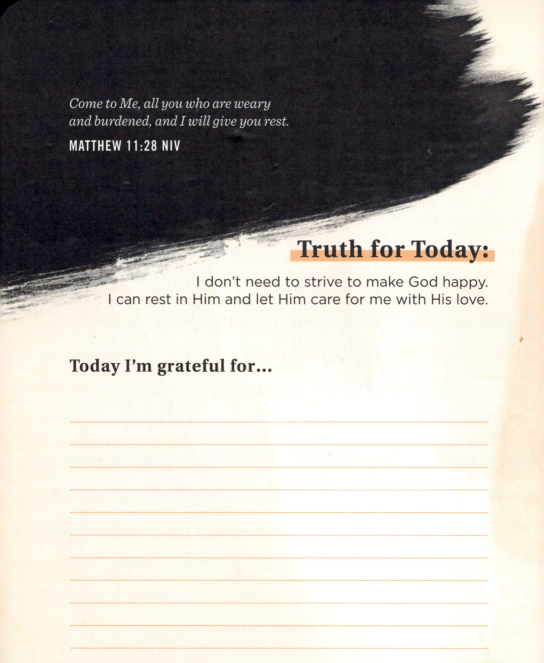

Come to Me, all you who are weary
and burdened, and I will give you rest.

MATTHEW 11:28 NIV

Truth for Today:

I don't need to strive to make God happy.
I can rest in Him and let Him care for me with His love.

Today I'm grateful for...

My prayer requests...

God doesn't want us to do more for Him. He longs to take care of us and whisper words of love and peace.

BONNIE GRAY

Yet I am confident I will see the LORD's goodness while I am here in the land of the living.

PSALM 27:13 NLT

Truth for Today:

I am able to see God's goodness even in difficult and painful circumstances.

Today I'm grateful for...

_____
_____
_____
_____
_____
_____
_____
_____
_____
_____
_____
_____

My prayer requests...

_____

_____

_____

_____

_____

_____

_____

_____

_____

_____

_____

_____

_____

_____

_____

_____

_____

_____

Sometimes we must sing what we believe, not what we feel. We must sing what we know, not what we see.

CATHERINE SEGARS

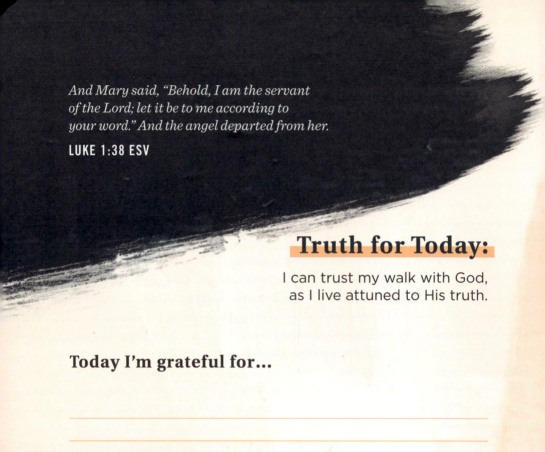

And Mary said, "Behold, I am the servant of the Lord; let it be to me according to your word." And the angel departed from her.

LUKE 1:38 ESV

Truth for Today:

I can trust my walk with God, as I live attuned to His truth.

Today I'm grateful for...

_____

_____

_____

_____

_____

_____

_____

_____

_____

_____

_____

_____

My prayer requests...

We don't have to worry about what's next—God is next. God is our steady. That is the beauty of a life tuned to His truth.

JENNIFER UECKERT

I am weary with my moaning; every night I flood my bed with tears; I drench my couch with my weeping.

PSALM 6:6 ESV

Truth for Today:

Lament is biblical and a gift for hurting hearts. I can lean into lament, giving my pain to God, and knowing that He hears and cares for me.

Today I'm grateful for...

_____

_____

_____

_____

_____

_____

_____

_____

_____

_____

_____

_____

My prayer requests...

_____
_____
_____
_____
_____
_____
_____
_____
_____
_____
_____
_____
_____
_____
_____
_____
_____
_____

*Pouring out my heart to God
allows me to experience hope
while I am still in the suffering.*

FAITH GRIFFIN SIMS

So if the Son sets you free,
you are free through and through.

JOHN 8:36 THE MESSAGE

Truth for Today:

Jesus will teach me what is true,
over and over again, and I can cling to that truth.

Today I'm grateful for...

_____

_____

_____

_____

_____

_____

_____

_____

_____

_____

_____

_____

_____

My prayer requests...

*Shame does not decide who
I am. Jesus has set me free.*

ALIZA LATTA

*Now faith is confidence in what we hope
for and assurance about what we do not see.*

HEBREWS 11:1 NIV

Truth for Today:

I can trust God, stepping out in
faith for that which I cannot see.

Today I'm grateful for...

_____

_____

_____

_____

_____

_____

_____

_____

_____

_____

_____

_____

_____

My prayer requests...

_____

_____

_____

_____

_____

_____

_____

_____

_____

_____

_____

_____

_____

_____

_____

_____

_____

*Faith is a reality
that can be trusted.*

LUCRETIA BERRY

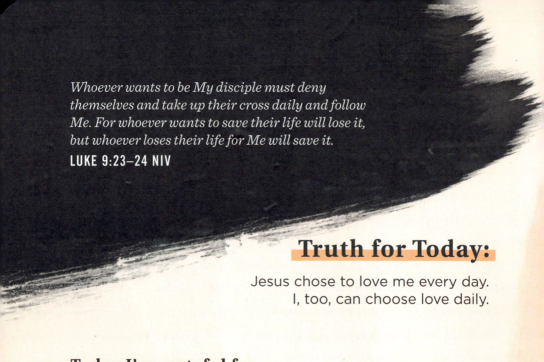

Whoever wants to be My disciple must deny themselves and take up their cross daily and follow Me. For whoever wants to save their life will lose it, but whoever loses their life for Me will save it.

LUKE 9:23–24 NIV

Truth for Today:

Jesus chose to love me every day.
I, too, can choose love daily.

Today I'm grateful for...

_____

_____

_____

_____

_____

_____

_____

_____

_____

_____

_____

_____

_____

My prayer requests...

To find what your heart needs
most is to take up the day's
cross, grab Jesus's hand, and
follow Him wherever He goes.

MICHELE CUSHATT

Share each other's burdens, and in this way obey the law of Christ.

GALATIANS 6:2 NLT

Truth for Today:

It's a blessing to be in community, sharing burdens and celebrations alike.

Today I'm grateful for...

_____

_____

_____

_____

_____

_____

_____

_____

_____

_____

_____

_____

My prayer requests...

_____
_____
_____
_____
_____
_____
_____
_____
_____
_____
_____
_____
_____
_____
_____
_____
_____
_____
_____

*This is church. It's you and me,
bearing burdens, celebrating
victories, and trading recipes.*

SHANNAN MARTIN

Just as our bodies have many parts and each part has a special function, so it is with Christ's body. We are many parts of one body, and we all belong to each other.

ROMANS 12:4–5 NLT

Truth for Today:

God is the creator of family, and there's room enough for us all in His family.

Today I'm grateful for...

_____

_____

_____

_____

_____

_____

_____

_____

_____

_____

_____

_____

My prayer requests...

The thing about being one of God's children is that when you're in, you're in for life... and then forever. You're never family-less.

ANNA E. RENDELL

He makes me lie down in green pastures, He leads me
beside quiet waters, He refreshes my soul. He guides
me along the right paths for His name's sake.
Even though I walk through the darkest valley,
I will fear no evil, for You are with me; Your rod
and Your staff, they comfort me.

PSALM 23:2–4 NIV

Truth for Today:

I can crawl to the feet of the Lord,
lie down, and He will comfort my heart.

Today I'm grateful for...

_____

_____

_____

_____

_____

_____

_____

_____

_____

_____

_____

_____

_____

_____

My prayer requests...

_____
_____
_____
_____
_____
_____
_____
_____
_____
_____
_____
_____
_____
_____
_____
_____
_____

There's only one place to restore
our soul and find comfort, and that's
in the quiet place at Jesus' feet,
where it's okay to not be okay.

KRISTEN WELCH

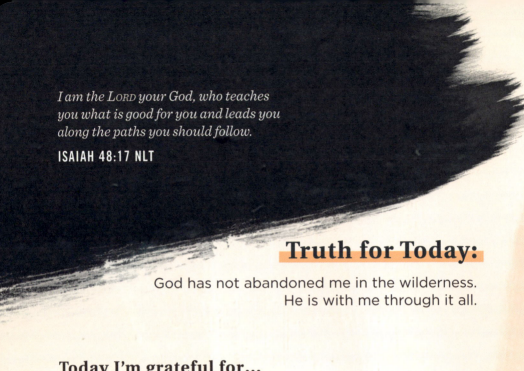

*I am the L*ORD *your God, who teaches*
you what is good for you and leads you
along the paths you should follow.

ISAIAH 48:17 NLT

Truth for Today:

God has not abandoned me in the wilderness.
He is with me through it all.

Today I'm grateful for...

My prayer requests...

Even in the wilderness, you're walking the path toward your promised land and it is an adventure between you and God.

STEPHANIE BRYANT

For when I am weak,
then I am strong.

II CORINTHIANS 12:10 NIV

Truth for Today:

I can give my hurt to the
Lord and rely on His strength.

Today I'm grateful for...

_____
_____
_____
_____
_____
_____
_____
_____
_____
_____
_____
_____
_____
_____

My prayer requests...

In His love we build bridges, not walls. That is what the world needs.

PATRICIA RAYBON

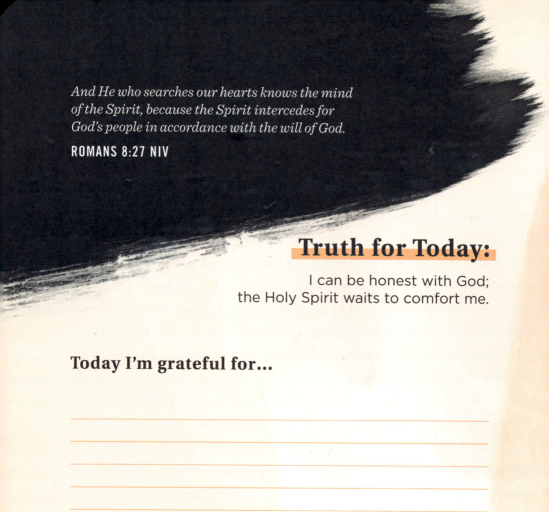

And He who searches our hearts knows the mind of the Spirit, because the Spirit intercedes for God's people in accordance with the will of God.

ROMANS 8:27 NIV

Truth for Today:

I can be honest with God; the Holy Spirit waits to comfort me.

Today I'm grateful for...

My prayer requests...

Tell God how you really
feel. God can handle your
full range of emotions.

TICCOA LEISTER

(in)courage welcomes you

to a place where authentic, brave women connect deeply with God and others. Founded in 2009 by DaySpring, the Christian products subsidiary of Hallmark Cards, Inc., (in)courage is a vibrant online community that reaches thousands of women every day. Through the power of shared stories and meaningful resources, (in)courage celebrates the strength Jesus gives to live out our calling as God's daughters. Together we build community, celebrate diversity, **and become women of courage.**

Join us at **www.incourage.me**
& connect with us on social media!

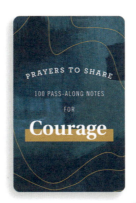

We hope you found peace, joy, and comfort in your journaling experience.

Looking for more from the (in)courage community?

Visit their website at **incourage.me** and be sure to check out the entire Take Heart collection at your favorite retailer or DaySpring.com.

Take Heart: A Prayer Journal
Copyright 2020 © DaySpring Cards, Inc.
Second Edition, November 2020

Published by:

21154 Highway 16 East
Siloam Springs, AR 72761
dayspring.com

Cover Design by: Becca Barnett
Written and compiled by: Anna Rendell

Printed in China
Prime: J2417
ISBN: 978-1-64454-808-0